THE BIRTHDAY PARTY

FIONA PRAGOFF

J. M. Dent & Sons Ltd
London & Melbourne

Fiona and Christopher are twins, and today is their birthday. They are five years old. All their best friends are invited to their birthday party.

And look! Everyone has brought a present for the twins. The doorbell rings. Abracadabra the magician has arrived. But what's that she's holding?

Abracadabra and the children go into the garden to play. Running round the magician they first play statues.

Next they play their favourite
game of pass-the-parcel.

Look what Martin has won:
gigantic sunglasses!

But now it's time for tea.
Abracadabra leads them all inside.

What a delicious feast!

Each of the twins has a cake: a train for
Christopher, and a clown for Fiona. It's hard
work blowing out five candles in one breath . . .

After tea Abracadabra shows the children some
exciting magic tricks.

She even lets them stroke the rabbit.
They all dance to music. Then they play
blind-man's-buff.

Now for the treasure hunt . . .
Hidden in the garden there is a present for
every child.
What do you think James has found?

Look: it's a jumping frog! Tina has a yellow parasol.

Rayna has a notebook.

All too soon it's time to go home.
Martin and Jo wave goodbye to the twins.

When everyone has gone Fiona and Christopher
open one last present each from their parents.

But what are these?

Puppies! One for Fiona and one for Christopher,
with smart leather leads for both of them.
Oh, what a wonderful birthday party!